Space Explorers

STARS

First Published in Great Britain in 2020 by Buttercup Publishing Ltd.
46 Syon Lane, Isleworth, Greater London, TW7 5NQ, UK

Author: Andrea Kaczmarek
Illustrator: Alexandra Colombo
Series Editor: Kirsty Taylor

A Cataloguing-in-Publishing record for this book is available from the British Library.

ISBN: 978-1-912422-90-6

www.buttercuppublishing.co.uk
contact@buttercuppublishing.co.uk
Printed and bound in China

2

"I love that our spaceship has so many silver stars above it, Grandpa." Daisy said as she stared out of her window at the bright night sky. The spaceship that she shared with her twin, Dan, was her most favourite possession. They both liked it so much, that they even named it after themselves 'COSMODAISYDAN'.

Grandpa smiled down at Daisy, "I think it is time for another adventure, don't you, science explorer? This time, let's look at the stars."

The twins were so excited. They loved going on space adventures with Grandpa and they couldn't wait to learn more. "But Grandpa, we need a clear, dark night to see the stars, don't we?" questioned Daisy.

"Yeah Grandpa, and what about COSMODAISYDAN? And the big, red telescope? They are both at your house!" shouted Dan.

Grandpa laughed at the twins. He was happy to see that they were learning a lot of from their missions. "True, but tonight, we will do things a little differently. We can take a big, warm blanket into the garden and watch the stars from there."

The twins were surprised. "No spaceship and no telescope? But how can we learn about the stars without them?" they asked.

"Wait and see my little science explorers. First, you both need to nap. I'll wake you when the sky is clearer. That's when our mission will begin!"

The twins were desperate to know more, but they knew that Grandpa was right. They definitely needed a nap! Space exploration was tiring work after all.

Daisy and Dan both went to their beds, eagerly awaiting their next mission.

Time passed and the sky was clear. Grandpa gently woke the twins. The three of them made their way to the garden. "I've cut out lots of silver star shapes, Grandpa." Daisy said, as she spread them out across the big, fluffy blanket.

11

The twins sat comfortably, staring up at the sky. Grandpa had brought his smaller telescope with him earlier that day. It too was staring up at the stars.

"They're beautiful, Daisy. But stars aren't actually that shape. They also aren't really silver. They can be all sorts of colours!" Grandpa beamed.

13

"Lie back, science explorers and look up at the sky." The twins did exactly as Grandpa said. "Which is the biggest star?"

The twins stared long and hard at the twinkling night sky. Dan shouted, "That one, up there! That's pretty big! Well, at least I think it is ..."

North Star

Grandpa nodded his head, "Yes, that is a big star. It's called the North Star. Travellers like the North Star as it helps them to find their way if they're lost. It will always be in the North."

Dan couldn't stop grinning. He got something right and Daisy didn't. That rarely happened.

"But the star I'm thinking of is much bigger. We don't really call it a star at all. We call it the sun ..." Grandpa continued.

Sun

The twins frowned as they stared hard into the night at the millions of twinkling lights shining down on them.

"The sun?" Daisy laughed. "But the sun is orange—"
"—or yellow," interrupted Dan.

Daisy glared at her twin brother before continuing, "And it keeps us nice and warm in the summer when the Earth is close to it. That's what you told us, Grandpa. It also only comes out in the day!"

"Indeed, I did." Grandpa chuckled as Daisy looked up at him grumpily. He was pleased that they both had been listening and had learned so much. "The sun is a star that is close to Earth. Look up at the sky at the other stars. Many of those are suns, too. But they are very, very far away. That's why they look so small.

He continued, "Stars are really just giant balls of dust and gas." Dan tried to stifle a giggle at the word 'gas'. Daisy rolled her eyes at him, "Not that kind of gas, Dan."

Grandpa coughed, "They get bigger and hotter and become stars. They come in all different colours too."

Dan looked through the telescope. "What colours can you see, science explorer?" Grandpa asked.

"A RED STAR! I CAN SEE A RED STAR!" Dan shouted.

"Well done, Dan." Grandpa said, patting him on the shoulder. "There are red and yellow stars up in the sky. Sometimes we can even see a blue star. They look quite small to us right now, but actually, they're gigantic. It's Daisy's turn now."

"Hhmm, I think I can see a yellow star, but it looks more silver to me." Daisy said as she searched the sky. She picked up the stars that she had made and placed them over the end of the telescope.

"It does look that way, doesn't it?" Grandpa agreed. "Staring up at the stars, we can see millions of beautiful little silver lights. But now you know the truth, I think it is time to explore some more."

"How many stars can you see?" Grandpa asked.

Daisy and Dan rolled around on the floor giggling, "We can't possibly count them all Grandpa! As you said, there are millions!"

Grandpa joined in, "Just try! I want you to see how big the galaxy is."

"What is a galaxy, Grandpa?" Dan asked.

"A galaxy is a group of stars, clouds of gas and lots of dust." Grandpa explained. Dan tried to stop himself from giggling again at the word 'gas'.
"There are millions of galaxies out there but the one that we live in is called the Milky Way."

The twins were silent, and they were never silent. "Wow!" they exclaimed. "So, Earth is part of a Galaxy called the Milky Way? Along with lots of stars?" Daisy asked.

"That's just the start, Daisy. But I'll save the rest for another time." Grandpa smiled..

The three of them went back to the fluffy rug and counted the stars. After a long time, the twins grew tired. They couldn't count any more. "There are hundreds, and hundreds, and hundreds …" Dan said, his eyes drooping with tiredness.

"There are thousands, and thousands, and thousands ..."
said Daisy, trying to stop a yawn.

Grandpa chuckled and put a spare blanket over the twins. He whispered to them
gently, "There are millions and millions, and counting them is a good way to get little
science explorers off to sleep ..."

30

"In the infinite sky, there is a bright star, I love you Kay to the moon and back"

with love
Alexandra Colombo